First Printing: 2016, Portacle Publishing

ISBN-13: 978-1540724922

ISBN-10: 1540724921

The

PROVERBS 4:7

GOLDEN GUM BALL

Because...

Relationships Matter

Table of Contents

The Purpose … Relationships Matter

Imagine living in a world of people who love each other and all get along.

Relationships Matter. Anyone can go purchase a gum ball, The idea of putting a coin in a gum ball machine and receiving a gum ball is simply a transaction. To obtain the Golden Gum Ball is to understand that relationships matter more then the product or service one may provide.

Prosperity and I mean **true prosperity** is a result of being relational with others while you transact futures.

Often we get the order reversed, and become transactional. ***The key is to be relational first, and also include the transaction.*** My friend Ford Taylor coined the term ***"Relactional"***. The idea is to relax and build solid relationships and then trust so that the transactions will follow. In short build quality relationships and own the Gum Ball machines,

RELAXIONAL:

An entrepreneur that is brilliant will combine the skill of relational excellence into the process of transacting quality solutions, simply they are a serving leader, that once the product or service is delivered, the other party will delight in rewarding or compensating you.

The point is that you need to relax, and transact business at the same time, this is the difference between an ordinary gum ball, that is hollow, than the one that is filled with quality substance. When you treat everyone with love and affection you create "Relational Equity". "Relational Equity" is the currency of the eternal, it lasts forever.

Dedication (Donald J. Trump)

I dedicate this book, _The Golden Gum Ball_, to Donald J. Trump and his family, a refined family who represent our great nation as First Family, because Family Matters. You are filled with the Holy Spirit, and not an ordinary gum ball, one that is empty and gets spit out. You are golden, a golden child, and a man of God and a producer of an excellent family.

Much like King Christian who used to ride daily through the streets of Copenhagen unaccompanied while the people stood and waved to him. One apocryphal story relates that one day, a German soldier remarked to a young boy that he found it odd that the king would ride with no bodyguard. The boy reportedly replied, "All of Denmark is his bodyguard."[1] We the citizens of The United States of America will guard you as a treasure as you conduct the Family Business to ensure our country is safe, and the business of our nation is conducted with excellence as we honor your position of Commander in Chief.

What honors us as a nation most, is that you Mr. Trump would enter the campaign as a wrecking ball, destroying much of the sewage that corrupts a nation to expose the Golden roads that pave heaven. You have inspired real hope, embraced Israel and you represent "We The People" Thank you for taking our nation back to it's Godly foundation, the foundation of truth that includes **POWER and INFLUENCE**.

I believe you will not see eye to eye with past presidents, simply because you are taller, in stature and in wisdom. You are the second tallest president, and will be the most powerful president the United States has ever seen because you understand the principles that govern authority and clearly understand the need for Godly Counsel. You are humble, reverent and qualified to lead our great nation to prosper.

---

[1] Wikipedia

I bless you and your presidency as we together take on the Apostolic call to do the Greater things, one of which is to make America Great again and to disciple Nations.

I decree you a Father of fathers, a Bishop to bishops, a lord, king and a warrior.

You will empower world class movements to increase righteousness, create biblical prosperity and alter the direction of nations to know Christ.

Significantly, Billy Graham prophetically declared that the next great move of God would come from the business community, you are affirming that as legitimate.

His son, Franklin said, "I believe it was God. God showed up. He answered the prayers of hundreds of thousands of people across this land that have been praying for this country."

On behalf of America, and the World, we appreciate and value you.

The Parable (The Golden Gum Ball)

"Boy, what are you, anyway?" It was not meant for a question, but, to the woman's surprise, the boy answered, frankly, simply:— "Father says that I'm one little instrument in the great Orchestra of Life, and that I must see to it that I'm always in tune, and don't drag or hit false notes."

"My land!" breathed the woman, dropping back in her chair, her eyes fixed on the boy.[2]

A stunning powerful statement of influence was the response of David when asked a rhetorical question. The Golden Gum ball is a sequel to the profound and moving book that saved my life.

I grew up in dysfunction and had to learn what it takes to live a life with **POWER and INFLUENCE**.

If you can imagine a very emotionally sick boy reading a book that would forever change his life, that was me. Life has a way of leading us at times to what I call the Golden Gum Ball.

So what is the Golden Gum Ball and why should you care? It is the essence of life, the only way to have ultimate victory.

In these pages I invite you to a greater understanding of what it means to live with **POWER and INFLUENCE**.

---

[2] Porter, Eleanor (2004-07-01). Just David [with Biographical Introduction] (p. 22). Neeland Media LLC. Kindle Edition.

THE GOLDEN GUM BALL: because ..."Relationships Matter"

I was twelve years old when I discovered the secret to ultimate freedom. I grew up in chaos, a broken family and nearly no peace. It was only by the divine hand of an Almighty God that I was fortunate to encounter the book that would save my life.

Love was absent in our home, and as long as I remained quiet and did what I was told, I would be able to live at my Grandmothers house. She was a conflicted woman who never really grew up. We might label her as dramatic and self centered. Dorothy was a victim to everything and a victor of practically nothing. Prior to understanding her condition, one might wonder if she was under the demonic influence of Satan, or that perhaps she was just a sociopath. In any event, she sure was not a very nice lady.

I remember specifically discovering the book, *Just David.* As I read the book, it was as if I moved back in time and found my buddy. The missing inner-child, known as David.

Ironically my middle name is Davis, and I have since decided to adopt David as my middle name because he goes with me and we play all the time.

To some of you reading this for the first time, it may come across as a bit odd or unusual as though what I am about to share were impossible, yet as you understand the Golden Gum Ball, I can assure you things will become clear.

So, I reached for the book and had a sensation that touched me from heaven, a sensation where I was at peace and harmony with God. Perhaps it was my guardian angel who lead and directed me to this relationship with David. I had no idea when I touched that book, he would become the Golden Gum ball through which I would understand wisdom and truth.

David invited me to the top of the mountain where real **POWER and INFLUENCE** reside. It was at the top of this mountain we became friends. David is my mentor, he teaches me everything. My first lesson from my best friend was that I had a Father and I was not an orphan. Unlike my natural family, one of whom was placed in foster care, the other sent to private school because my Grandmother was too selfish to love anyone but herself.

David introduced me to my future adopted father, although I did have a natural father. My natural father was broken, he was not really able to understand me, like David's father did. David's father adopted me and helped me understand love. My only sadness, is that I only had a short time with my adopted father.

David and I enjoyed playing and were best friends on the top of the mountain. The view was tremendous and it was the safest place I have ever been. Absolutely nobody would ever leave that safe haven on a voluntary basis, yet his dad said it was time we moved down to the valley. Neither David or I wanted to leave, yet we had to honor our father and journey down to the valley where the mean people lived. There were no mean people on top of the mountain, and David taught me that there is a safe place where you can have joy and peace, this was his secret place.

I remember noticing David's dad, my adopted father as we walked down the mountain, he seemed to not be able to keep up and I imagined that he was just tired, I guess you get that way as you get older. This was where the journey got real. I looked over at David, and said; What are you doing David? David looked over at me with his blissful smile, and picked up a squirrel that was laying on the ground. David showed it to our dad and asked, "What is wrong with the squirrel?" Our dad answered, "Well David that is no longer a squirrel, that is the earth suit that the squirrel left behind." David, I noticed got some water in his eyes as if he had somehow become very sad. Our father said, "David this is a happy moment, that squirrel is running around in heaven, he is very happy to be released. I looked over at David, I saw his sadness turn to Joy.

The journey to the valley was packed full of lessons, of which each moment was a treasure that would ultimately point to the Golden Gum Ball. At some point as we journeyed David shared how he so enjoyed the view from the top of the mountain, especially the "silver lake", it was his favorite and most serene experience. David pointed to the lake, and shared how the lake made him feel peaceful and centered, except he knew it was going to be his last time viewing it. It was as if David just knew things, and had an intuition about futures. David looked at me, grabbed me by the arm and swung me toward the "Silver Lake" and said, Did you see that? Did you see the Sun, it turned the "Silver Lake into Gold"? He was so excited to share this new discovery, it was as though it was a sign from the Creator. That is when I realized something different, it was as if I could hear David, but David could no longer hear me.

I was screaming at the top of my lungs...DAVID!

It was as if I fell off the side of the mountain and my eyes were opened, my Grandmother was standing over my bed, and viciously tore the book from my hands. She then told me to get up and go sit in the corner. *Evidently that was her book, and she was outraged that I would dare to read that book with-out her permission.* Then she forced me to memorize the bible as punishment. Reading the bible was not so fun because it was always what I had to do when I got punished. That day was a bad day because after being forced to read, she then made me learn how to spell. As a little boy, she terrified me, and was relentless that I learn. This style of teaching only lead to my unconscious rebellion. She berated me and forced me to spell simple words. I remember not being able to spell the word, T-H-E. After a few failed attempts, she screamed to my father, "John! JOHN! you need to spank him" , Sadly, he spanked me because I was unable to spell, then placed me in the corner where it was extremely cold for hours till it was time to go to bed.

Just before going to bed, I snuck into the kitchen and found the flashlight. Even though I was punished, I really wanted to speak with my friend David. After the lights went out, I softly walked over to the book shelf and picked up the book. I got under the covers with my flashlight and started reading.

David and I moved from the mountain to the valley.

Up there, too, the sun still shone, doubtless,—at least there were the rose-glow and the Silver Lake to look at, while down here there was nothing, nothing but gray shadows, a long dreary road, and a straggling house or two in sight. From above, the valley might look to be a fairyland of loveliness, but in reality it was nothing but a dismal waste of gloom, decided David.[3]

When I finally caught up to David, I noticed that his father was not doing so well. He actually fell along side the road, and as I looked around I saw David standing, talking to a lady at a nearby home. The lady did not seem to be so nice and then I heard the door slam in David's face. "David, what is going on?" I asked. He then asked me, "What is a Tramp?" It astonished me, David had no idea what it meant to be labeled. I then defined what a tramp is.

TRAMP:
A person who travels from place to place and does not have a home or much money. [4]

David responded, ***"I am no tramp, who would say such a thing."*** I thought to myself, evidently David has never been to the valley before. As we dialoged I helped David to understand that even though we were walking through the valley, we would be safe. I think he experienced fear for the first time. I was just glad to be with him and a part of the journey to comfort him.

The next thing I knew, that same lady evidently got some conscious awareness that her behavior was a bit rude and she miraculously opened the door and offered David some food for him and our father.

"See here, boy," began the woman, looking out at him a little less unkindly, "if you're hungry I'll give you some milk and bread. Go around to the back porch and I'll get it for you." And she shut the door again. David's hand dropped to his side. The red still stayed on his face and neck, however, and that fierce new something within him bade him refuse to take food from this woman.... But there was his father—his poor father, who was so tired; and there was his own stomach clamoring to be fed. No, he could not refuse. And with slow steps and

---

[3] Porter, Eleanor (2004-07-01). Just David [with Biographical Introduction] (p. 13). Neeland Media LLC. Kindle Edition.

[4] Merriam-Webster Dictionary.

hanging head David went around the corner of the house to the rear. As the half-loaf of bread and the pail of milk were placed in his hands, David remembered suddenly that in the village store on the mountain, his father paid money for his food. David was glad, now, that he had those gold-pieces in his pocket, for he could pay money. Instantly his head came up. Once more erect with self-respect, he shifted his burdens to one hand and thrust the other into his pocket. A moment later he presented on his outstretched palm a shining disk of gold. "Will you take this, to pay, please, for the bread and milk?" he asked proudly.

The woman began to shake her head; but, as her eyes fell on the money, she started, and bent closer to examine it. The next instant she jerked herself upright with an angry exclamation. "It's gold! A ten-dollar gold-piece! So you're a thief, too, are you, as well as a tramp? Humph! Well, I guess you don't need this then," she finished sharply, snatching the bread and the pail of milk from the boy's hand. The next moment David stood alone on the doorstep, with the sound of a quickly thrown bolt in his ears. A thief! David knew little of thieves, but he knew what they were.[5]

I watched David as a real sadness over took him, it was as though he was grieved.   I asked David, Why are you so troubled? David Said; The Valley is tough, and on the mountain it is much more pleasurable.   You see, on the Mountain there is kindness, gentleness, self control and much love. **The people in the valley just need what we have on the mountain.** I then asked him why he thinks things are so difficult in the valley. David Explained; The Valley is where the people have permitted each other to act unkindly, and in the valley people make lower choices because the valley is a territory where the Ruler of the earth, has been given permission to the enemy of our soul to create chaos and discord.

Once you have lived on the mountain and know harmony, you have been gifted the Golden Gum Ball, to bring harmony where discord lives. David explained that when you have experienced true **POWER and INFLUENCE.** , you become a steward of those gifts, and have

---

[5] Porter, Eleanor (2004-07-01). Just David [with Biographical Introduction] (p. 14). Neeland Media LLC. Kindle Edition.

a responsibility to model the best behavior to others. I was quite interested in how David just seemed to brush off the labels, as if they had no impact so I asked. David. why don't you deal with that lady when she insults you and labels you like that, doesn't it bother you that she is acting rude? David said, *"I have learned that true character does not defend, justify or blame others. Most people do not respond, they react."* I asked; David why are you so kind and gentle to someone that does not deserve it?" David said; *"Compassion is gift that guides our life, it is actually two words, Compass and Passion, that when you put them together you operate at high levels of personal Power and generational Influence."*

It was as if I was in a time warp, I was in the valley with David one moment, the next I was in excruciating pain. Old Dorothy was at it again, this time she was smacking me with a heavy broomstick. There she was standing over my bed smacking me relentlessly. Evidently I fell asleep with the book, and she caught me. This time it was worse then ever. The welts from the broomstick turned to bruises.

Not a fun way to awaken, yet it was my reality. I knew that day if I did not cover the bruises, when I got home from school, there would be more inflicted. What I wondered mostly is how could this woman be so hurtful, what happened to her that she was so shallow?

After returning from school, knowing I was in trouble, I tried to avoid Dorothy, except she was not having anything to do with my avoidance. She stood at the door when I arrived and told me that I had ruined her life, I was an imposition and not wanted. She was very crafty with her words and her insults - that as a little boy, I just believed her.

I could not believe that Dorothy made that book more important than me. It was as though that book was somehow more important than my feelings, and my life. It was hard to understand that the only way I would be good enough for Dorothy is to simply obey her rules, opposed to her sharing her book. She made things more important than people, all the time. It was as though I was a TRANSACTION, opposed to being a real person.

What happens to people that are treated like a transaction opposed to being treated with value and worth, people rebel. "Rules without relationships lead to rebellion." The phrase was coined by Josh McDowel

Dorothy, I often refer to her as "BIG Dorothy", took my book, so I was grounded and could not connect with my friend David. It was hard living in the valley of the shadow of death with Dorothy. You just never knew when you were going to be punished, and for what.

I remember eating some of her Planter Peanuts. She was so angry when she figured out that I ate her peanuts, she literally hit the floor and started crying like a big baby. She even embellished her dissatisfaction by improvising the situation with extreme drama. She pretended to have a heart attack as though she was dying, then she said she was going to have my stomach pumped out to get her peanuts back. As a little boy, I believed her and was on the way to call the hospital, when she miraculously got healthy and evidently had a moment of amnesia regarding her promise to have my stomach pumped out.

I really missed David. I knew that our adventure was on pause, and one day we would be reunited. Until then, I was stuck learning on my own. Having grown up in a small town and still being a kid, I had a few adventures without David that were noteworthy.

One such adventure related to a Gum Ball machine. While the Gum Ball machine did not have a Golden Gum Ball, it had one very nice prize in the middle of all the others. The prize was a zippo lighter with the American flag on it. It was a long shot, but I wanted to win that prize. I remember that summer working hard and mowing lawns. Every time I received a few dollars, I would convert them to quarters. I bought all the prizes above the special lighter (Golden Gum Ball), until finally out it came. I had FINALLY received the prize.

It seemed to me that all the other trinkets were not the same as the zippo lighter with the American flag. They were the transaction, but the lighter was GOLDEN.

I really wanted to tell David about my amazing prize. I knew if I hunted that eventually I would find the book, and reconnect with my best friend.

One day Big Dorothy had to go play cards with her gambling buddies, and this gave me the time and space to find my friend. Sure enough, I found my book and reconnected with David.

I yelled, "Hey David", and he looked around and we connected.   "Where have you been?", exclaimed David. I told him about the valley experiences with Dorothy, and the mountain top experience when I received the Golden Zippo lighter.

We laughed and then we were back on track, as if no time had elapsed.

David quickly brought me up to speed, that my adopted Father was not doing so well and they just needed a resting place.

Little did I know David found a barn where he and our father could sleep. It was a comfortable place and an honor to journey with David in this most special time. Our dad asked David to play the violin, a gift that they both enjoyed together.   They were magnificent musicians, and when they played together you could hear the harmony of heaven. This time, David played alone at the direction of our father. I suppose it was a very serene moment. I knew that this was a very special request because it was as though our dad had no more energy to play, and that David was ushering in real Angels to walk his father to heaven. The sound of heaven permeated in the room, it was a very special time, then I saw what seemed to be like a white and purple smoke released in the air, then our father was at peace.

Suddenly the owner of the barn showed up…

"Boy, what do you mean by playing a jig on your fiddle at such a time as this?" "Why, father asked me to play" returned the boy cheerily. "He said he could walk through green forests then, with the ripple of brooks in his ears, and that the birds and the squirrels—" "See here, boy, who are you?" cut in the man sternly. "Where did you come from?" "From home, sir."

"Where is that?" "Why, home, sir, where I live. In the mountains, 'way up, up, up—oh, so far up! And there's such a big, big sky, so much nicer than down here."[6]

Ohh no! I heard Big Dorthy come through the kitchen door, quickly I told David, "Got to go...." then I shut the book and put it back on the shelf. I immediately went to the corner of the house where I was supposed to stay, and just pretended to be a good little boy. This pleased Big Dorothy.

Whenever Big Dorothy left for her gambling addiction, I would reconnect with David. He was clearly my best friend, and we somehow needed each other. He was brilliant, creative and a wonderful friend, someone I could trust.

The real challenge for us was time, the issue I began to notice is that I kept getting older, and David remained the same age. He never got older, and I began to realize that maybe our friendship was not even real. I started believing that this was all just in my imagination.

I made one more visit to David, then I would not talk to him till I was over 40 years old.

"Hey David" I yelled. David as usual was excited to see me. He sure was a great friend. A friend that sticks closer then a brother for sure.

David shared the following letter that our father wrote:

David, my boy, in the far country I am waiting for you. Do not grieve, for that will grieve me. I shall not return, but some day you will come to me, your violin at your chin, and the bow drawn across the strings to greet me. See that it tells me of the beautiful world you have left—

---

6 Porter, Eleanor (2004-07-01). Just David [with Biographical Introduction] (pp. 18-19). Neeland Media LLC. Kindle Edition.

for it is a beautiful world, David; never forget that. And if sometime you are tempted to think it is not a beautiful world, just remember that you yourself can make it beautiful if you will.

You are among new faces, surrounded by things and people that are strange to you. Some of them you will not understand; some of them you may not like. But do not fear, David, and do not plead to go back to the hills. Remember this, my boy,—in your violin lie all the things you long for. You have only to play, and the broad skies of your mountain home will be over you, and the dear friends and comrades of your mountain forests will be about you.   DADDY. [7]

Suddenly after hearing the letter, I realized that Big Dorthy was close by, I slammed the book. Something inside me changed that day, I realized the love of a father to a son. I knew that day I had a loving father, yet felt something missing.

It was my 16th birthday, I was nearly a man. I will remember this day for the rest of my life,. It was a day of liberation. I remember being done with the manipulation of Big Dorthy and it was time for me to be a man.   The incident happened around a dispute.   I went to the refrigerator to drink some milk, and Big Dorothy substituted real milk with powder milk.   This was not acceptable. I said, "Look it Dorthy, if you ever substitute real milk with powdered milk I will sell your antiques. and purchase real milk." This idea was outrageous to Dorthy, an act of rebellion at the highest order. She was no longer able to throw her temper tantrums, and now that I was bigger then her, she could no longer physically abuse me, so she played her last card.   It was an ACE, she called the police and had me removed from the home.   That evening it was cold, thank God I had my own car for shelter.   I took my stuff and decided to live in my car. It was a long cold night, a lesson learned.   *I never ever felt home there, and would never return.*

For years relationships were only transactions.   You put in the quarter, you get the Gum Ball.   The problem is that once the sugar is removed, you spit out the waste.   That is how I treated the world. Relationships were disposable.

---

[7] Porter, Eleanor (2004-07-01). Just David [with Biographical Introduction] (p. 33). Neeland Media LLC. Kindle Edition.

I felt like an orphan with no real friends.   It was a lonely journey.

Dorthy died, my natural father died, and I did indeed sell the antiques. That day I think I might have gone and purchased a milkshake as way of celebration for selling the antiques as promised.

In the debris while selling the antiques, I found my book. David was waiting for me. At first I thought how ridiculous of me to believe the fantasy that I could have a real friend, someone who loved me and treated me with respect and dignity. This idea was just a fantasy.

I took the book and laid it on my shelf.

It was my 40th birthday when I decided to pick up the book and get reacquainted with David and my adopted Father.

Honestly, when I opened the book and saw David, he was actually quite angry. I said, "Hey David." He looked at me and to my shock and surprise he said, "Where have you been?" "I am angry at you!" at first I wanted to shut the book and just forget ever knowing David. I knew in my heart he was sharp, wise and certainly able to speak into my life, yet as an adult I felt a bit challenged having a conversation with a little boy from a fictitious book.

I took a deep breath, and remained open to the conversation. David said, "Why did you leave me, don't you even know who I am?" I was perplexed, actually I had no answer. Then his anger seemed to escalate, he was extremely angry and needed some answers. He said, "What did I do, that made you leave me, you ABANDONED me!"   At this stage of the conversation I wanted to slam the book and have nothing to do with him. Then he said… "Do you want to leave me here? Forever. WHY!" I felt a bit ridiculous but I decided to answer him, "David, you did not do anything wrong, I abandoned you because I was afraid." "Afraid of what?" David expressed.   I said, I was afraid you were not real. Then he told me everything I ever needed to know, he said, "I am your little boy, the one you abandoned, the one you let go of and rejected, I miss you and want to know if you are going to leave me here." I at 40 years old started to weep uncontrollably, as David moved off the pages of the book and hugged me. It was a reunion of sorts, I had rescued my little boy. I had somehow repossessed my childhood and I had reunited with my little boy, the one who liked to play, trusted people, had faith to do greater things and was my special gift, that Golden Gum Ball, the missing piece. Finally William "David" Winship, was whole and together. I also remembered my adopted father, the one who demonstrated unconditional love, the one who gave me that compass, the one with real passion, Compassion.

Then David asked me to enter his world as he showed me one more very special thing, my future.

"Father, where in Heaven's name DID you get that boy?" he demanded. "Who taught him to play like that? I've been trying to find out from him, but I'd defy Sherlock Holmes himself to make head or tail of the sort of lingo he talks, about mountain homes and the Orchestra of Life! Father, what DOES it mean?"[8]

The gift is the Golden Gum Ball. It is the one Gum Ball that is not empty. You cannot chew it up, you will not spit it out, it is Jesus Christ, the Gift is the Holy Spirit of God that empowers you to know all truth NOW, it is the gift that empowers you to higher achievement. This is the secret, Jesus Christ.

David remains my best friend, my middle name, my most trusted advisor. It is the King in me, Jesus Christ, the King of kings, the Lord of lords.

I now bless you to discover more about *The Golden Gum Ball because... "Relationships Matter"*.

---

[8] Porter, Eleanor (2004-07-01). Just David [with Biographical Introduction] (p. 178). Neeland Media LLC. Kindle Edition.

Success is synonymous with the use of Power and Significance is synonymous with being Influential, achievement is reliant on your ability to negotiate and navigate well.

All power comes from God, the issue is that not all power is safely distributed. As an example you may have "**Positional Power**" as the CEO of your company, and instead of prizing relationships, you may treat your staff, employees and even customers with disrespect, or minimize their value by lording over them because you are in a position.   Just remember that your position does not necessarily true authority.   It is possible to use a position in a manner that is a bit sparky, opposed to dispersing power well.

Personal Power relates to your personality, gifts, knowledge, education and competency. This power is useless when we fail to understand our counterpart. It is critical we meet people where they are and that we understand and meet their needs.   The best practice is to model behaviors that you want others to resemble, or to be a serving leader.   Personal power that inspires others will create high trust.

Perhaps the highest form of power is, **Relational Power that focuses on interdependence.**   Cracking the code to high achievement, requires two vital elements; Navigating Power with Influence and Negotiating Success and Significance. The key is to understand that "Relationships Matter", and I mean every relationship you form or do not form matters.   Life's achievement often comes down to reputation and/or your character.   *People do business with* *people they trust, they remain in business with people of character and follow people who have a passion to do the greater things.*

High achievers are committed to continuous improvement, they have an anchor that is deeply planted in principle centered living, they negotiate with buoyancy, and manage their power brilliantly. Achievers focus on the mission of life, most particularly they understand that "Relationships Matter".

Focus produces profit, there is profit in the process of continuous improvement. In our book, _Winship Rules_ we speak about the importance of remaining in the channel where success and significance exist. The channel markers are **Profit and Order.** When you do only those things that create order and invest in only those things that create profit, you position yourself, family, business and community in a place where safe power exists.

In short, Relationships drive profit, we are in an economy that relies on relational excellence. It is the pearl of **GREAT VALUE,** the merchant saw that changed his life. He was willing to sell everything to get that pearl. That pearl is essentially a genuine relationship with God, the source of all power. Knowing your source is the essential truth that gives you the ability to negotiate and navigate a life filled with eternal power so that you leave a legacy of leadership in your wake.

David, the Golden Gum ball was filled with the Holy Spirit. His brilliance was because he understood power, he understood that even though we walk in the valley, our light can shine in the darkness and displace rude, and hurtful behavior. His humility, grace, kindness, and championship victorious attitude, understood that there was more power with people than to power over people. His child like faith was the essence of his nature, the true nature of high achievers. He became what his father spoke over his life.

David was an amazing instrument in the great Orchestra of Life, and he created harmony where ever he went, often displacing discord, my best friend the Holy Spirit.

William D. Winship is the CEO of Portacle™ and an **Architect of Righteous Power.** He is recognized for his 3 and 5 day Relational Excellence Practical and Custom Organizational Assessment tools that help to eliminate dysfunction in business and personal lives.

The work we do is integrated with the 5 dysfunctions of a team, to align a person, marriage, family, organization and community to continuous improvement by focusing on fresh habit formation to include the 5 habits of a cohesive team.

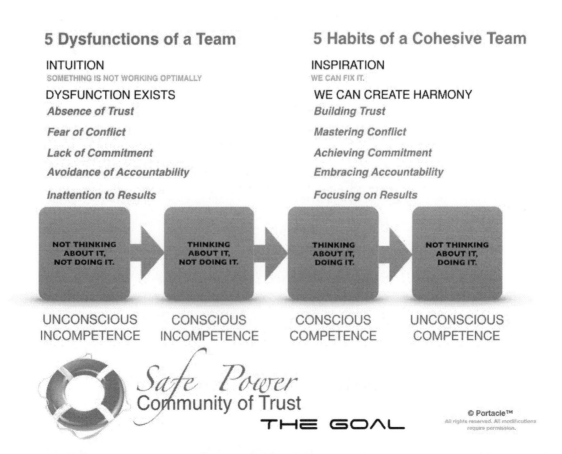

5 Dysfunctions of a Team

INTUITION
SOMETHING IS NOT WORKING OPTIMALLY
DYSFUNCTION EXISTS
Absence of Trust

Fear of Conflict

Lack of Commitment

Avoidance of Accountability

Inattention to Results

5 Habits of a Cohesive Team

INSPIRATION
WE CAN FIX IT.
WE CAN CREATE HARMONY
Building Trust

Mastering Conflict

Achieving Commitment

Embracing Accountability

Focusing on Results

NOT THINKING ABOUT IT, NOT DOING IT.	THINKING ABOUT IT, NOT DOING IT.	THINKING ABOUT IT, DOING IT.	NOT THINKING ABOUT IT, DOING IT.
UNCONSCIOUS INCOMPETENCE	CONSCIOUS INCOMPETENCE	CONSCIOUS COMPETENCE	UNCONSCIOUS COMPETENCE

Safe Power
Community of Trust

THE GOAL

Psalm 23

God, my shepherd!

I don't need a thing.

You have bedded me down in lush meadows,

you find me quiet pools to drink from.

True to your word,

you let me catch my breath

and send me in the right direction.

Even when the way goes through

Death Valley,

I'm not afraid

when you walk at my side.

Your trusty shepherd's crook

makes me feel secure.

You serve me a six-course dinner

right in front of my enemies.

You revive my drooping head;

my cup brims with blessing.

Your beauty and love chase after me

every day of my life.

I'm back home in the house of God

for the rest of my life.

Jesus Christ, the Anchor of my Soul..

"Thank you, Jimmy."

THE GOLDEN GUM BALL: because ..."*Relationships Matter*"

"Observe people who are good at their work— skilled workers are always in demand and admired; they don't take a backseat to anyone."

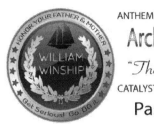

ANTHEM

Architect of Righteous Power

"*The Science to Profit by Design*"

CATALYST

Passion, Trust & Character

Printed in Great
Britain
by Amazon